CW01267160

OFF·WE·GO

Swimming

Gillian Mercer
Illustrated by Frank Endersby

Technical consultant: Carol A. Hicks

Kingfisher Books

Parents: these notes are for you.

Swimming is fun, good exercise and essential for water safety. The earlier your child becomes familiar with water the better.

Babies can start coming to the pool from around four to five months, or at least three weeks after their first immunization. You may like to join a parent and baby class, especially if you don't feel very confident in the water yourself. If your child enjoys splashing in the water at bathtime, first swimming lessons could start at three, but don't expect too much at this early age. Classes for the under-fives concentrate on building up their confidence in the water before they learn the proper strokes, and usually last between half and three quarters of an hour. Disabled children will particularly enjoy the sense of buoyancy and mobility in the water. Many classes welcome all children, but check first that your teacher is qualified to work with disabled children.

Kingfisher Books, Grisewood & Dempsey Ltd
Elsley House, 24–30 Great Titchfield Street, London W1P 7AD

First published in 1990 by Kingfisher Books

Text copyright © Gillian Mercer 1990
Illustrations copyright © Grisewood & Dempsey Ltd 1990
All rights reserved

BRITISH LIBRARY CATALOGUING IN PUBLICATION DATA
Mercer, Gillian
　Swimming.
　1. Swimming – Manuals – For children
　I. Title　II. Endersby, Frank　III. Series
　797.2'1
ISBN 0 86272 531 3

Edited by Camilla Hallinan
Cover design by The Pinpoint Design Company
Colour separations by Scantrans Pte Ltd, Singapore
Phototypeset by Southern Positives and Negatives (SPAN)
Printed in Spain

CONTENTS

At the pool	4
What to take	6
Getting in	8
First exercises	10
Breathing	12
Underwater	14
Kicking	15
Afloat	16
Gliding	18
A stroke to practise	19
Splash!	20
At the seaside	22
What next?	24

Swimming pools are noisy, splashy and lots of fun.

This is the babies' class. Your class is next.

• At the pool •

Don't take a baby or young child to the pool if they are unwell. And always remember safety rules: be sure to watch children at all times, even when they can swim a little; and teach them not to run and not to push, for their own safety and for others'.

5

• *What to take* •

You need to bring your swimsuit, or swimming trunks, and a nice big fluffy towel.

Now you are ready to change.

• *What to take* •

Inflatable armbands are useful buoyancy aids, but you needn't let your child become dependent on them; always ensure time in the water without them. Choose good quality armbands with double chambers and safety valves. They should be worn above the elbow and should fit well. You can gradually reduce the air as your child gains confidence.

Your can bring your favourite bathtime toy.

SHOWERS ↑

POOL →

7

• *Getting in* •

The teacher calls out everyone's names.

Parents sit and watch the lesson. They like to see what you are doing.

Parents are often encouraged to watch the class – you will enjoy your child's progress and you can help keep an eye on his or her safety in the pool.

• Getting in •

The first thing you'll learn is how to get in.

Walk down the shallow steps, or come backwards down the ladder, till your feet touch the bottom. The water feels lovely and warm.

Here's a useful way of getting out.

Hold on to the edge, with your elbows up, lift one leg up onto the edge, and pull yourself out.

• First exercises •

"One at a time, jump in,"
says the teacher.
SPLASH!

When you get in,
hold on to the edge
of the pool and walk along.

Can you run races
through the water?

Or jump like a frog?

• First exercises •

You can sing a noisy song while you splash:

*Here we go round the mulberry bush,
The mulberry bush, the mulberry bush;
Here we go round the mulberry bush
On a cold and frosty morning.*

*This is the way we wash our face,
Wash our face, wash our face;
This is the way we wash our face
On a cold and frosty morning.*

*This is the way we dip our heads . . .
This is the way we jump up and down . . .*

11

• *Breathing* •

When your face is in the water, you blow bubbles to breathe out and to stop water going up your nose.

Watch how the teacher blows bubbles through the water. Try it with your face down in the water. You can practise this in the bath at home.

• *Breathing* •

Now everybody practises bobbing up and down in the water.

*Ring-a-ring o' roses,
A pocket full of posies;
A-tishoo! A-tishoo!
We all fall DOWN.*

• *Underwater* •

It's fun to go right down underwater. Hold your breath and try to keep your eyes open.
You can pretend to be a big fish.

Can you pick up a toy
from the bottom of the pool?

• *Kicking* •

Now for some real work! Listen hard to what the teacher is saying.

First, try this exercise.

Hold on to the rail. Stretch out and kick up and down.

15

• Afloat •

Floats hold you up in the water so you can begin to swim. Start with two floats like this.

Kick with nice straight legs and floppy feet. Keep your chin on the water.

You can go quite fast!

Now try with one float.

The floats help you swim on your back too. Look up at the ceiling and keep your tummy up as you kick.

• *Afloat* •

When you want to stop and stand up in the water, you bring your knees under your tummy and push your legs down to the bottom.

If you are on your back, you draw your knees up to your tummy, lift your head up and push down.

• *Gliding* •

Now, can you swim without any floats?

Push out from the edge
and stretch out your arms
like Superman flying.
How far can you glide?

Throw a toy to the
middle of the pool and
see if you can reach it.
Start kicking and soon you'll be able
to get all the way across the pool.

• *A stroke to practise* •

Here is an arm movement to practise:

stretch your arm right out in front, then pull it back through the water and up again.

Try this stroke again, with the other arm.

Swimmers need lots of practice.

> Don't worry if your child can't swim yet. Visits to the pool should above all be fun – too much pressure may unnerve the reluctant swimmer.

• Splash! •

Time for one more jump before you go home.
SPLASH!

Here is a game to play at the end of the class.

Old Macdonald had a pond,
E-I-E-I-O.
And on that pond he had a . . .

E-I-E-I-O.

swan **dragonfly**

duck

frog

Children should leave the pool before they become tired or cold. Dry quickly and thoroughly, and wrap up in warm clothes – a hot drink is a good idea too.

sea horse

fish

whale

seal

With a splash-splash here,
A splash-splash there,
Here a splash, there a splash,
Everywhere a splash-splash.
Old Macdonald had a pond,
E-I-E-I-O.

• *At the seaside* •

The seaside is even more fun when you can swim.

• At the seaside •

Everyone enjoys a day at the seaside, but remember – young children are not yet strong swimmers. So always take care when you are on the beach or near a river, pond or pool.

23

• What next? •

For details of swimming lessons near you, consult your local library, swimming pool or leisure centre, or telephone the Local Authority. The following organizations should also be able to help:

Amateur Swimming Association
Harold Fern House
Derby Square
Loughborough
Leicestershire LE11 0AL

The ASA train swimming teachers (check that your instructor is suitably qualified) and runs a Rainbow proficiency award scheme for children. The first badge in the series is the Puffin badge for swimming five metres with a buoyancy aid. There are also awards for other water skills such as floating and treading water.

Association of Swimming Therapy
4 Oak Street
Shrewsbury
Shropshire SY3 7RH

British Sports Association for the Disabled
The Mary Glen Haigh Suite
34 Osnaburgh Street
London NW1 3ND

National Association of Swimming Clubs for the Handicapped
St George's House
Coventry Road
Coleshill
Birmingham B46 3ED

Sports Council
16 Upper Woburn Place
London WC1H 0PQ

Royal Life Saving Society UK
Mountbatten House
Studley
Warwickshire B80 7NN

Contact the Society (telephone 052 7853943) for details of their Water Safety Award and Aquapack, a comprehensive safety programme for young children.

Water Safety Advisor
Royal Society for the Prevention of Accidents
Cannon House
The Priory Queensway
Birmingham B4 6BS

Other books to read
For children:

Going Swimming
Heather Amery and Peter Ingham *Usborne*

Going Swimming
Celia Berridge *Kingfisher Books*

Harry by the Sea
Gene Zion and Margaret Bloy Graham *Picture Puffin*

Lucy and Tom at the Seaside
Shirley Hughes *Picture Corgi*

Spot Goes on Holiday
Eric Hill *Picture Puffin*

For parents:

Teach Your Child to Swim
Susan Meredith with
Carol Hicks and Jackie Stephens
Usborne